# BUSING: CONSTRUCTIVE OR DIVISIVE?

✺

Virginia Trotter, *Moderator*

✺

Nathan Glazer
Robert L. Green
Charles Morgan, Jr.
Orlando Patterson

**THE AMERICAN ENTERPRISE INSTITUTE FOR PUBLIC POLICY RESEARCH,** established in 1943, is a publicly supported, nonpartisan research and educational organization. Its purpose is to assist policy makers, scholars, businessmen, the press and the public by providing objective analysis of national and international issues. Views expressed in the institute's publications are those of the authors and do not necessarily reflect the views of the staff, advisory panels, officers or trustees of AEI.

## ADVISORY BOARD

Paul W. McCracken, *Chairman, Edmund Ezra Day University Professor of Business Administration, University of Michigan*

R. H. Coase, *Professor of Economics, University of Chicago*

Milton Friedman, *Paul S. Russell Distinguished Service Professor of Economics, University of Chicago*

Gottfried Haberler, *Resident Scholar, American Enterprise Institute for Public Policy Research*

C. Lowell Harriss, *Professor of Economics, Columbia University*

George Lenczowski, *Professor of Political Science, University of California, Berkeley*

Robert A. Nisbet, *Albert Schweitzer Professor of the Humanities, Columbia University*

James A. Robinson, *President, University of West Florida*

## EXECUTIVE COMMITTEE

Herman J. Schmidt
*Chairman of the Board*
William J. Baroody
*President*
Charles T. Fisher III
*Treasurer*
Richard J. Farrell
Richard D. Wood
Richard B. Madden

## SENIOR STAFF

Anne Brunsdale
*Director of Publications*
Joseph G. Butts
*Director of Legislative Analysis*
Robert B. Helms
*Director of Health Policy Studies*
Thomas F. Johnson
*Director of Research*
Gary L. Jones
*Assistant to the President for Administration*
Richard M. Lee
*Director of Planning and Development*
Edward J. Mitchell
*Director, National Energy Studies*
W. S. Moore
*Director of Legal Policy Studies*
Robert J. Pranger
*Director of Foreign and Defense Policy Studies*
Louis M. Thompson, Jr.
*Assistant to the President for Communication*
David G. Tuerck
*Director, Center for Research on Advertising*

# BUSING: CONSTRUCTIVE OR DIVISIVE?

Virginia Trotter, *Moderator*

Nathan Glazer
Robert L. Green
Charles Morgan, Jr.
Orlando Patterson

A Round Table held on March 18, 1976
and sponsored by the
American Enterprise Institute for Public Policy Research
Washington, D.C.

THIS PAMPHLET CONTAINS THE PROCEEDINGS OF
ONE OF A SERIES OF AEI ROUND TABLE DISCUSSIONS.
THE ROUND TABLE OFFERS A MEDIUM FOR
INFORMAL EXCHANGES OF IDEAS ON CURRENT POLICY PROBLEMS
OF NATIONAL AND INTERNATIONAL IMPORT.
AS PART OF AEI'S PROGRAM OF PROVIDING OPPORTUNITIES
FOR THE PRESENTATION OF COMPETING VIEWS,
IT SERVES TO ENHANCE THE PROSPECT
THAT DECISIONS WITHIN OUR DEMOCRACY WILL BE BASED
ON A MORE INFORMED PUBLIC OPINION.
AEI ROUND TABLES ARE ALSO AVAILABLE ON
AUDIO AND COLOR-VIDEO CASSETTES.

© 1976 BY AMERICAN ENTERPRISE INSTITUTE
FOR PUBLIC POLICY RESEARCH, WASHINGTON, D.C.
PERMISSION TO QUOTE FROM
OR REPRODUCE MATERIALS IN THIS PUBLICATION IS GRANTED
WHEN DUE ACKNOWLEDGMENT IS MADE.

ISBN 0-8447-2071-2
LIBRARY OF CONGRESS CATALOG CARD NUMBER 76-21974

*PRINTED IN UNITED STATES OF AMERICA*

LC
214.5
B87

VIRGINIA TROTTER, assistant secretary for education, Department of Health, Education and Welfare, and moderator of the Round Table: Is mandatory busing to bring about school desegregation constructive, or is it divisive? The controversy surrounding this question does not arise because of dangers or problems for students caused by bus transportation per se. It arises because of what mandatory busing represents, and that is the desegregation of the public schools by forces beyond the direct control of parents. The problem is generally not even that parents resent desegregation as a social objective. By and large, they seem to resent desegregation only when it requires their children to attend schools that are not of their own choice.

Considered from the viewpoint of the parents, this is understandable. Yet, the constitutional mandate of equal opportunity could not be clearer. In instances where injustices have occurred because of racial discrimination, it is essential that these injustices be eliminated. The courts have said that, as a last resort, segregation of schools has to be eliminated by lengthy bus rides. The conflict between the obligation of the courts to eliminate segregation and the desires of the parents to control the institutions and the social forces affecting their children is the topic of our discussion here today.

To illuminate the question before our panel, let us first turn to Robert L. Green. Dr. Green, is busing productive or counterproductive in terms of educational quality?

ROBERT GREEN, dean, College of Urban Development, Michigan State University: First, I think we should be very clear about one point: 20 million American children are bused annually, and only a very small minority—less than 4 percent—are bused for the purposes of racial integration.

Now, to answer the question, there is a body of data to support the point of view that busing can be productive and supportive of a high degree of educational quality.

In the instances and cases in which busing has been a mechanism to facilitate school desegregation, there is evidence that when parents do not interfere and community groups are not organized or opposed to the integration of schools by busing, then school children—given the opportunity to learn, to grow, and to develop together—do so with a very minimum of conflict.

DR. TROTTER: Dr. Glazer, is busing effective public policy, in terms of the actual amount of integration that is achieved through this method?

NATHAN GLAZER, professor of education and sociology, Harvard University: What I have in mind when I talk about busing is not busing, which is obviously unobjectionable, but the involuntary assignment of students to schools on the basis of race. This is what I object to.

I think, on the whole, that busing has been irrelevant to issues of education. It's neither facilitated education, nor made it more difficult. Effective education depends on all sorts of other circumstances. Busing is not instituted to improve education, and one wouldn't expect it to. It has been instituted for other reasons, which I suppose we'll get into. And I think, in many circumstances, it's been sufficiently disruptive, combined with other forces, to say, "Well, it certainly hasn't been a good idea."

DR. TROTTER: Mr. Morgan, is there a difference between the North and the South, in terms of the appropriateness of busing as a means of desegregation?

CHARLES MORGAN, director, Washington Office, American Civil Liberties Union: I think there is. I don't think there's a southerner, white or black, who all during the years of the civil rights movement didn't think, just as George Wallace said, that once it got to South Boston and the souths of the North that the white liberals would retreat.

DR. TROTTER: Dr. Patterson, to what extent do you think the blacks have benefitted from school busing?

ORLANDO PATTERSON, professor of sociology, Harvard University: The problem is—benefitted in what respect? I think part of the confusion lies in the fact that there is little agreement concerning what the exact goals of busing might be.

To some extent, most people are concerned with direct educational benefits. Increasingly, however, people are asking, even assuming that there are educational gains, what are the implications of these educational gains?

And the weight of sociological evidence here is rather pessimistic, because the structure of income inequality in America is such that education itself makes relatively little difference to the pattern of inequality, as well as to the pattern of unemployment, and so on.

It seems to me, too, that one has to consider the benefits in social terms. One could make a good case for busing as a means of increasing the level of communication between the races in the United States. As someone who is a non-American, I find it really quite extraordinary that, after being together for several centuries in this country, there should be such awkwardness, even on the public level, in terms of racial interaction.

So, there are different kinds of benefits, and quite often these benefits conflict with each other. We have to be clear on which ones we have in mind and which we consider to be most important.

MR. MORGAN: Blacks, unlike Jews and other ethnic groups, came to this country as slaves, were subjugated as slaves, and were made the subject of the Thirteenth, Fourteenth, and Fifteenth amendments—which were written not for the rights of women and others, even though I've used them for such cases, but were written solely for the rights of blacks, as an affirmative mandate on the government to correct racial inequality and its results.

I stress that because you've raised certain questions about blacks and whites not interacting, and that sort of thing. Does that not take the whole problem of blacks in America out of the context of ethnic minorities and ethnic group thinking? Is any of the rhetoric we hear about busing that compares it to the plight of the Jews or of the Poles or of the Italian-Americans—does it apply to blacks at all?

DR. GREEN: In response to Professor Glazer, I think that much of the desegregation and litigation nationally has had as its focus the improvement of educational quality. As a part of that, strategies related to remedy have been sought.

And in order to bring young people together for purposes of racial integration and in order to improve quality —first in terms of academic achievement, and second in terms of communication and the breaking down of racial attitudes that impact negatively on how young people view each other very early in life and in later life—there has been a very specific focus. Busing is only a strategy to bring that process about.

I think the critics of busing should come up with an alternative. And I have discovered that those who are opposed to utilizing busing as a strategy to desegregate American schools have brought forth no other strategy. If not buses, you could use airplanes, helicopters, trains—

MR. MORGAN: Gondolas. [Laughter.]

DR. GLAZER: Well, we've agreed that the means of transportation—in fact, even the issue of transportation—are not in question. In my mind, the issue is involuntary assignment by race, which brings me, if I may comment briefly—

DR. GREEN: I'd like to respond.

4

DR. GLAZER: Certainly.

DR. GREEN: On the matter of involuntary assignment, that really is not a good argument, because we find, for example, that very often young people who are physically handicapped, with spinal disorders, paraplegics, one arm, no arms, one leg, no legs, no arms, no legs, have no choice as to where they attend school. In some counties, they ride buses ten, twelve, fourteen miles per day, and their parents do not oppose it. As a matter of fact, parents are very upset if the buses are late or do not run.

So the question of involuntary assignment is only an issue when race is involved. And I think—

DR. GLAZER: Well—

DR. GREEN: Let me finish my point. On that score, we talk about forced busing, but we never talk about forced schooling. We force youngsters to attend school for the first sixteen years of their lives in states throughout the Union—even Arkansas and Alabama now force kids to attend school until they're sixteen—but we don't talk about forced schooling—

MR. MORGAN: What do you mean, "even Alabama"? [Laughter.]

DR. GREEN: Even Michigan.

DR. GLAZER: And Mississippi.

DR. GREEN: Even Boston.

DR. GLAZER: Right.

DR. GREEN: But my point is this. Terms such as "involuntary assignment" and "busing" only become prominent in the minds of Americans when questions of race and social class are raised. So I think somewhere along in this discussion, we need to focus upon race, race bias and social class bias, too.

DR. GLAZER: I'm glad you added the social class issue—

DR. GREEN: Yes, social class bias as we see it in Boston.
Not until the issues are honestly addressed will we focus on matters that are important. We can't ignore the fact that busing in America is widely accepted and widely endorsed. In my state of Michigan, busing is supported to the tune of millions, but very little of this busing is done for the purposes of racial integration.

DR. GLAZER: Well, I think we will be addressing those questions. But I wanted to take up, just briefly, Mr. Morgan's point about the special position of blacks—and I fully agree with that point as he put it. However, how do we deal with the following problem: In the North or the West, where there are very large minorities aside from blacks, no government or court order, it seems, can limit itself to blacks. No order can be predicated on the position that because blacks happen to be a group with special legal status in the United States, the status of having been slaves and having had laws addressed to them, the order need concern itself only with blacks.

In San Francisco, there are the Chinese, the Japanese, the Nicaraguans and the Spanish-surnamed, and all the school children are classified into four groups and are being moved all over the city—to no particular avail, to my mind. In Boston, too, you would think that blacks and whites would be enough. But no, we have yet a third category of utter confusion, which is "others," and we also had to decide whether the Chinese are minority or not minority —I forget how we decided it—and then we have to decide what to do with the Puerto Ricans, and so on.

In other words, we are really dealing, to my mind, with a spreading plague, in which ethnic and racial categorization is more and more fixed on people through governmental action, through the action of courts.

Now, admittedly, this is not the reason why South Boston is up in arms. I don't believe that they are concerned about the theoretical constitutional issue. And I understand that. But I must say that I am concerned about it. I'm concerned about a nation which more and more writes ethnic and racial categories into its law. I thought we got rid of that in 1964, and I hoped that would be final.

But admittedly, there is a second issue that we have to get to, one that Dr. Green is raising—if busing itself is not the reason people are up in arms, then what are the reasons? And that leads us to the race and social class issue.

MR. MORGAN: I think what you're referring to now is the use of racial statistics, of those kinds of group identifications or individual identifications in our society by government; am I correct?

DR. GLAZER: Right.

MR. MORGAN: Now, when we began in 1879 or 1880 to strike down statutes that excluded blacks from juries—the Supreme Court said those statutes were no good—white public officials in the South immediately started practicing exclusion without statutes. They just left blacks off.

Over the years, when blacks were convicted, they'd raised the question of systematic exclusion from juries. They couldn't prove that they were left off for a racial reason, because the white officials came in and said, "We didn't do it for that reason." Now, the way statistics came up was as follows: The courts said, "Look, if 80 percent of the population in this county is black, and no black has ever served on a jury, the burden of proof shifts to the state or to the county; they have to prove that blacks were *not* excluded because of their race." They never could prove that. So racial statistics came to be used as a technique of proof.

Second, with respect to that technique of proof, when we started suing affirmatively to desegregate schools, juries, and so on, the court, after it made a specific finding that there was racial discrimination, said the only way the defendant could prove nondiscrimination was to present statistics showing black participation equivalent to the percentage of blacks in the general population.

Now, that's where the rule comes from. It doesn't come from the Department of Health, Education and Welfare or anyplace else. It comes simply from a rule of evidence. After discrimination is proved, then comes what is now referred to as quotas.

DR. TROTTER: I'd like to know whether you think there is ever a time when busing is not fair, or when it is inappropriate in terms of racial integration.

DR. PATTERSON: You see, there is still the assumption in this discussion that busing is good per se. I think we ought to recognize that it works in certain circumstances, but not in others. Even more important, we should begin to specify exactly what we're speaking about.

One must begin thinking in cost-benefit terms. Now, let's take the issue of busing as a means of simply creating a more civilized situation between the races—which, for me, is one of the major justifications for busing. Does it work? Is the cost too great? Now, let's take the Boston situation. I find it extraordinary that blacks—among the most impoverished groups in Boston, economically and socially—should be bused to the most impoverished group among the whites, socially, culturally and economically. If blacks are going to be bused I should think it would have been a more rational approach to bus them to a middle-class neighborhood.

MR. MORGAN: Of course.

DR. PATTERSON: One of the problems, you see, is that the white lower classes, who are the most impoverished whites socially and culturally, are being asked to bear the burden of busing. And frankly, I cannot see the benefits for the black child.

MR. MORGAN: That's precisely correct. I don't think you're going to get any disagreement out of either of us.

DR. PATTERSON: All right. Now, continuing with analyses of social benefits, assuming that we do bus children into middle-class neighborhoods, is there proof that busing improves the nature of the relationship between the races?

Now, I've always assumed that it does, but I've also read data—

DR. TROTTER: There is some.

DR. GREEN: There is some civil rights data from 1966, indicating that blacks and whites who attend integrated, multiracial classrooms very early in life are more likely and are more willing to select friends from the opposite perceived racial or cultural group as adults.

I think we're at the point now where we have a very unique opportunity to collect data in a wide range of school districts—North, South, East and West—looking not only at race, but social class as well, in terms of attitudinal change over time.

The difficulty that social scientists encounter, unlike their natural science counterparts, is the fact that very often the data related to attitudes on school desegregation must be collected in a very tense, highly conflictual situation. And so the collection of data often is very difficult.

But looking at it from another standpoint, there is a body of data that supports the point of view in several school districts, from California to Michigan, that the desegregation of schools does improve educational quality. That's another cost-benefit.

DR. GLAZER: Under what circumstances, though? You know, I recall, for example, that the New York private schools in the early sixties were trying to attract black children; they gave out scholarships here and there, and—

DR. GREEN: Everybody wanted one.

DR. GLAZER: They got up to two, three, ten, and so on. [Laughter.] And it was fine. Whites met blacks, and blacks met whites, and some of these kids maybe had better opportunities for getting into colleges and so on.

METCO,* in Boston, has been in existence now for seven or eight years, I suppose, and by now about—what

---

* Editor's note: Metropolitan Council for Educational Opportunity, Inc.

is the figure—either 1,500 or 2,500 black kids are bused to suburban schools. They go voluntarily, because they want to go or their parents want them to go. The communities they go to accept them, are happy to have them. I must say, in that circumstance, I don't care what the educational research shows.

Educational research is so difficult. It's very complicated and disputed. I mean, sometimes it shows that blacks have developed a negative self-image. I think probably all that means is that when black youngsters go out to these high-class Brookline and Newton schools, they discover they're not as smart as they thought they were—which is all right: it's a very useful thing for everybody to discover.

MR. MORGAN: Or, like some of us, they discovered when they went out there that the folks out there weren't as smart as they thought.

DR. GLAZER: That, too. The point is I don't care about the research in a situation where something which I approve of, integration, is happening on a voluntary basis.

On the other hand, first, my guess is that when busing takes place on a voluntary basis, it has to work out, whatever temporary, negative, or other effects there are. And because educational research is so ambiguous, I say here—even though I'm a professor—that I overrule it, and say that's a good thing.

But in other cases, particularly cases where there is—and now we get to our constitutional issue—great resistance, where people say, "I don't like it, I don't want it, nothing's going to happen as a result of it, and I didn't do it"—in those cases, it's not going to work out very well.

DR. GREEN: Well, I think, too, when we speak about voluntary transfer, freedom of choice, voluntary desegregation, the burden is very typically put upon the limited minority, the small minority, who are always at a disadvantage.

And I don't think we can talk about 2,500 black youngsters in an experimental program in Boston being bused out to upper-class white schools. We need to talk about the quarter of a million in Detroit, the vast numbers in San Francisco, New York, Chicago, Pittsburgh, and so forth. Also, 2,500 youngsters typically, on a voluntary basis, have no impact on national public policy in the area of education. What we need to address is the issue of public educational policy.

DR. TROTTER: This brings us back to the courts, and what is the proper role in terms of enforcing the law against discrimination.

DR. PATTERSON: Well, I want to emphasize that there cannot be a single policy on education for the whole country. What I fear is that a certain amount of dogmatism has evolved in this debate.

DR. GREEN: You would suggest policies for the North that would not be enforced in the South?

DR. PATTERSON: No, no. We're not talking about the North and the South. I'm just saying perhaps every situation—

DR. GREEN: We have equal protection of the laws; that's national policy.

DR. PATTERSON: To get back to the Boston situation—and I live in that situation—it seems to me that the cost in terms of violence, in terms of development of racial animosity—

DR. GREEN: But do you speak for Selma, Alabama? There was a tremendous amount of violence in Selma, Alabama; blacks were killed, white liberals from the North who came down were killed—

DR. GLAZER: Well, there, I think we do have to come back to that North-South question, which, I think, is very important. I know how it's presented—that the North was happy to impose this on the South and doesn't want to impose it on itself.

I think that the development of the law has obscured, to my mind, a really crucial distinction. On the one hand, you have de jure segregation—that is, when blacks and whites are separated by law. And when that is done, it's very effective. Oh, maybe a black passes here and there, but you really can do it 100 percent.

Then you have another situation—

MR. MORGAN: You can do it 100 percent with a high wall.

DR. GLAZER: That's right. Then you have another situation—de facto segregation—where they are not separated by law. Now, I'm giving you, admittedly, a judgment—my judgment, which still the courts disagree with—I just think they're wrong, that's all.

MR. MORGAN: You have your right.

DR. GLAZER: Right. In Boston, for example, there were very few, if any, 100 percent black schools. (There were none, incidentally, in San Francisco.) I would guess that about half of the black students in Boston were going to school with at least 10 or 20 percent whites. In other words, it was a much more mixed situation, with schools probably ranging from 100 percent black to zero black, with a lot concentrating around 80 or 90 percent black, and quite a few at 20 percent, and so on.

Now, in a situation like that, where there is mixing and where there is no history of legal segregation of the races, people are not aware that anybody is doing anything to them: the whites are not particularly aware that anyone is helping them keep out the blacks (and the blacks are not particularly aware that anyone is keeping them out). Maybe the Boston situation is a little different from the general Northern situation, but the fact is, it's a much more mixed situation than Selma. When you talk about Selma, I think you're talking about a situation of deliberate, recognized injustice, a radical effort in the case of

Selma to keep blacks from voting. There is no radical effort to keep blacks from voting in Boston; I think there never has been. Or, if there has, it's so long ago, nobody remembers when it was.

If it means violence to give blacks the right to vote or to break down the legal segregation of the races, then you need violence. But what is the violence in Boston for?

DR. GREEN: But you must remember that efforts must be made to control violence at every level, irrespective of whoever is involved in perpetuating violence.

I think the de facto, de jure argument that's being raised now is basically an artificial one. It doesn't matter that schools in Selma and other parts of the South were segregated by law and those in the North were segregated de facto. We find that the behaviors and policies of officials in cities like Detroit and states like Michigan and Illinois bring about the same result.

And as to your argument that white parents in Boston are not aware that there is a systematic effort to deny blacks due process, if that is the case, then those parents aren't very literate and aren't reading—because realtors and bankers all engage in a process to make sure that blacks live in racially segregated residential districts. It isn't necessary any more for them to hang out signs saying, "No blacks wanted."

There was a CBS special or NBC special a very short time ago on "redlining" and the systematic effort, even today, to keep blacks out of white areas, irrespective of income. I read a piece of yours, Dr. Glazer, in which you stated that income determines where blacks live. Sir, there's a tremendous body of data, part of which I have access to and would be willing to share with you, indicating that not income, nor education, but race and ethnicity are the most volatile factors in determining where blacks live in the United States of America.

DR. GLAZER: I think the point is that income certainly determines that in part, and the question is how big the part is.

MR. MORGAN: The real point is that, we can argue a variety of positions—either it's income or jobs, as Professor Patterson said, or it's housing or ethnicity or something else—but it doesn't much matter what it is. To make progress, you just start and you go, and it works out or it doesn't. If somebody wants to work on the job situation, that's fine with me; if somebody wants to work on the housing situation, fine.

But I think what I am hearing is a version of "Albert Schweitzer liberalism." I grew up around that sort of thing. It's the liberalism that says, "Send your old clothes and Albert Schweitzer to Africa, and worry about the poor starving Chinese." I have gained more pounds worrying about the poor starving Chinese. I know Selma is the "poor starving Chinese" to the folks at Harvard, and I know the same thing exists all across this country.

DR. GLAZER: I would still make a radical distinction.

DR. TROTTER: Let's get back to the question of what busing is doing to us. Is it divisive, or is it constructive? Is it necessary?

DR. GREEN: Busing is a neutral construct. People are divisive. Policies that are not enforced are divisive. Individuals who misunderstand others and the motivation of others are divisive.

Blacks and whites in South Boston and Roxbury who do not understand that their welfare rates are the same and that their high school dropout rates are equally high— they are divisive. (Actually for one month in late 1975 South Boston's welfare rate was slightly higher than Roxbury's.) Blacks and whites have to understand that their plight is a common one.

DR. PATTERSON: It seems to me, on that issue, that the only thing that busing has done is to make blacks and whites aware of—

DR. GREEN: Busing hasn't done that.

DR. PATTERSON: —the dividing line.

DR. GREEN: Busing is a strategy that will lead, we hope, to reeducation and the kind of learning process that you referred to, which will lead to—

MR. MORGAN: Integration, by the nature of the word, brings people together. Busing, as well as all sorts of other integration measures, makes some white folks very mad. When it makes them mad, then they say it's divisive. But the fact is busing just makes them mad. [Laughter.]

DR. GLAZER: May I suggest that busing is divisive among blacks, too. I testified in a suit that's just been completed in Cleveland—the judge has not given down his order—on the school integration issue. He's trying to find out if there's segregation.

MR. MORGAN: He can't just look and see?

DR. GLAZER: He's trying to find out if it's segregation caused by actions of the school board.
 Cleveland's school board is headed by a black man, Arnold Pinkney, who has run for mayor twice and lost, coming closer the second time than first. The previous mayor of Cleveland was also a black, Carl Stokes.
 As I was listening to the case, I looked at the two tables. The plaintiff's table was headed by Nat Jones of the NAACP and by my friend, Tom Atkins, from Boston—two outsiders (who, however, undoubtedly have some community support) arguing this case before a judge. The defense table was headed by a white lawyer, a Cleveland man, and sitting with him were a black Cleveland lawyer, the white school superintendent, black school officials, and so on. Their feeling was that they didn't think the way school children were distributed by race in Cleveland was the greatest thing in the world, but things had developed that way and it wasn't the fault of the school board.

MR. MORGAN: Natural order—black folks and white folks.

DR. GLAZER: No. Blacks came into Cleveland on the east side of town and expanded eastward. The city is divided by a substantial canyon, the Cuyahoga River, and the east side has gotten mostly black. The west side stays white. As blacks have moved up in the world, the east side has developed middle-class black sections, where the schools are middle-class schools.

The blacks are asking, "What's going on here?" What's going on is that somebody has decided that half the students in the west side ought to be bused to the east side, and half the students in the east side ought to be bused to the west side. And as far as I can see, an awful lot of the people from Cleveland don't see any purpose to this enterprise.

DR. GREEN: Things were seen the same way in the South. When blacks in department stores in the South couldn't try on clothing (black women had to purchase a dress and if they took it home and it didn't fit, they couldn't return it), when blacks and whites rode separate elevators in the department stores, when the NAACP began to file suits and when Martin Luther King, Jr., began to lead demonstrations, and so on—when these things were happening people were asking the same question that you're asking now.

DR. GLAZER: Well, there's a radical difference. In the South, one group was subordinate to the other.

DR. GREEN: But there are radical differences in Cleveland, in terms of reading scores, in terms of academic achievement. My colleagues at Stanford, at Harvard, and at other leading eastern institutions willingly joined me in examining school desegregation policies in Prince Edward County, Virginia, when I did my research there. Now that we're looking at northern urban institutions, many of the same colleagues—and I include many of the friends we know very well—are beginning to draw a very unfair comparison and a comparison that's essentially the same.

DR. TROTTER: What you're really talking about is how much difference does desegregation make in terms of the quality of the education our students receive.

DR. PATTERSON: Let's not get too involved with the details of the thing. There are some real issues: What is busing all about? What's the ultimate objective of all this steam that has been generated around the country?

It seems to me that once we begin to ask these basic questions, the issues turn out in a different way. If the long-term objective, the ultimate objective, is to reduce inequality, then I say busing is not the best way to go about it—

MR. MORGAN: What option do you have?

DR. GREEN: Give me some historical evidence of the options.

DR. PATTERSON: Wait a minute. Busing has a negative effect, in the sense that I think it's obscuring the basic issues. A great deal of the energies of black leaders—and of the liberals who should be their supporters—is directed at this issue when it should be directed at other issues.

MR. MORGAN: Name one.

DR. PATTERSON: The problem of the increasing, not the decreasing, unemployment—

DR. GREEN: We're working on that. There's a major full employment committee.

DR. PATTERSON: In terms of the allocation of leadership energies?

MR. MORGAN: What do you want me to do, sashay over to the White House and ask Gerald Ford to hire a bunch of black folks?

DR. PATTERSON: No, but you can exercise the same kind of political concern and interest—

DR. GREEN: It's being done. I can give you evidence that it's being done.

DR. PATTERSON: But there's no impact. All over the country the unemployment of blacks and young ethnics is increasing.

MR. MORGAN: The reason we're all here is that we were able to go to school and get an education. That's the reason you teach at Harvard—

DR. GREEN: And it makes a difference in your outcome, too.

MR. MORGAN: It happens that education is a weapon. I don't believe it's an end in itself, or an answer.

DR. PATTERSON: I don't think it's an effective weapon.

DR. GREEN: It certainly is; it's been a good one for centuries.

DR. GREEN: There are very few like yourself at Harvard—

DR. PATTERSON: The fact that what's true of myself— and I happened to be one of the lucky few—

DR. GREEN: Because of education.

DR. PATTERSON: Yes, but that doesn't mean that, even with education, everyone could make it, because the structure of inequality may be such that while several can make it at any given time, a substantial number will have to be losers, and that's what the issue goes to—

MR. MORGAN: Well then, let's not make the laws so that they guarantee that.

DR. GREEN: And don't minimize education. Instead, look at discrimination as a factor which prevents more from being at Harvard where you are, and at Michigan State where I am.

DR. GLAZER: I would like to get back to the educational issue. Dr. Green said something which is very potent. When I spoke of METCO and of the 2,500 black students who were being bused voluntarily, he said, "Well, that's nothing."

I think a lot of us don't realize how much voluntarism can do. I'd like to make this point: That 2,500 happens to be 10 percent of all the black students in Boston—there are a total of about 25,000 to 28,000. So, 10 percent voluntarily chose some other school. And of the others who chose not to be bused—leaving aside the mandatory busing that's going on today—an awful lot were already attending schools that were 20 or 30 percent white, which was integrated enough for them.

And I'm not suggesting that the 2,500 who chose to go to suburban schools made that choice because there were whites there; they were choosing to go to better schools.

I have seen evidence that if voluntary programs are available—and, admittedly, we haven't had them for places as big as Detroit, and that might be an interesting thing to try out—20 or 30 percent of the blacks will choose to join the program and accept some such burden as busing. A lot of them will do so because it's a better school or a school they want to go to. Catholics decide they want to go to a Catholic school, and they'll get on a bus; or people will decide that they prefer the high schools at the other end of town.

And I think that the notion that this is unfair, that people should have to do something to get something, is wrong. There's nothing wrong with that. Let people choose.

Now, if we have voluntarism, what about all those that decide not to participate? Here, I do want to say something for education. I know our experience isn't very good, but I just don't believe that the black school is an impossible school, despite the fact that a lot of kids have chosen something else. Let me make myself clear. Maybe it's an impossible school today; maybe they haven't yet figured out how to make it a better school. But I simply do not believe that there is something absolutely organic and essential in black culture that means that a predominantly black school—one that's black not because of the law but because of where people live—is going to be a lousy school.

MR. MORGAN: Let me ask you a question. Do you know of any instance in the history of this country—or, perhaps, any other—where white folks have put their money into schools their children haven't attended; and do you think black folks would if they had the money?

DR. GREEN: And related to that, weren't you raising the argument of separate but equal?

DR. GLAZER: I didn't put it that way.

DR. GREEN: Well, can blacks learn together in an all-black setting? I would say yes, in all-black nations. It can happen in Kenya or in Zaire. But as long as our society is as race conscious and class conscious as it is, then all-black schools will not function adequately in America, because forces are established to make sure that they do not function adequately.

As for voluntarism, it's always been interesting for me to note that those who hold power speak of voluntary behavior. Historically, that has always been the case.

When we are looking for ways to include those who are at a disadvantage, one good example is in Jerusalem. I spent some time in Israel a short time ago and visited schools throughout that country. There's a major busing project in Jerusalem designed to bring together the Sephardics and the Ashkenazis, the low-income and upper-middle income Jews, and to break down social class. That's not a voluntary project at all, sir. It's mandated by the Israeli minister of education.

DR. GLAZER: Well, let me still pursue the point. I think—

DR. TROTTER: What we're really talking about is how to find the kind of social balance that will do the best thing for each one of these students that we're busing or not busing.

DR. GLAZER: Well, that's yet another kind of issue.

I just want to make a distinction between conditions in Israel and conditions in the United States. I prefer voluntarism. I also see that Israel is a nation under siege that has a high morale—

DR. GREEN: The black community is under siege; poor people are under siege—

DR. GLAZER: Well, it's slightly different, though.

MR. MORGAN: Not just blacks, but poor people in our society—they are besieged, too, sir.

DR. GLAZER: What I'm saying is that I would argue that the United States is trying to get away from the notion that people should be moved around and deprived of one thing or another on the grounds of their race. I think that, on the whole, people don't like it. They also don't see where it's—

DR. GREEN: They just don't like busing for racial purposes. They support the busing of 20 million children, minus 4 percent.

DR. GLAZER: Yes, but that's because that busing is something they choose, they really choose.

DR. GREEN: But they like it. You said they didn't like it.

MR. MORGAN: Let me talk to you about choice for just one second.

DR. GLAZER: I'm saying people do not like the fact that because you are black or because you are white, you're going to have to do this—not because you're dumb or you're stupid or you need it or you have a bad back or you're handicapped, but just because you're black or white, just because you're Chinese or have a Spanish surname. I think we want to get away from that.

MR. MORGAN: Bob Green's experience and mine is from the South, so we start with a southern bias with respect to what we've seen and where we think this country is going. You've got to remember that some of us who were there knew that the Harvard Corporation was the largest stockholder in Mississippi Power and Light; we knew that United States Steel owned Birmingham, Alabama, lock, stock and mill, and we knew where the power centers were in the North, that they would not voluntarily move to make change, but they would make change because they were forced to in their own hometowns. Now, it's come home to their hometowns and to their suburbs, and they don't like it. White southerners understand that; black southerners understand that.

DR. GREEN: This is why blacks are supporting Jimmy Carter.

MR. MORGAN: That's also a reason why there is a great deal of prejudice in the North against Carter.

Now, let me just make one point about voluntarism. When you talk about people in buses, remember one thing about the situation of the black farmer in Greene County, Alabama. Farms are becoming giant corporate farms all over this country. The acreage of the country is going to the massive corporate farms, and to the timber, paper, and chemical companies. The blacks are being moved off the farms just as they get the right to vote and the right to serve on juries and the right to control their own lives. Now their kids may live in rural poverty, but that sure beats urban poverty, as I've seen it as I've gone north.

Black's aren't in Harlem, and they're not in Boston, and they're not in Michigan, and they're not in California because their move was voluntary. They'd probably rather live where they started, where they or their parents grew up. But the jobs are where they are. The unavailability of jobs and the unavailability of rights forced them off the land.

We talk about voluntary moving, voluntary busing and voluntary travel. Just remember, you do have a right to move in this country. But the real problem is—you don't have a right not to move.

DR. PATTERSON: I'm concerned about the lack of reality in this discussion. We're neglecting the political realities of the situation.

What this discussion boils down to is that we are hoping that essentially dependent institutions, plus moral suasion and the courts, can be effective weapons for improving ultimately both the relations between the races and the conditions of the poor. That is what worries me. Haven't we reached the limits; just in terms of the power and realities of the situation. Maybe the South could be kicked around because the South is a weaker part of the country.

I'm asking, have we reached the limits in terms of using legal institutions for attaining structural changes? And isn't there a possibility that by pushing the use of the courts too far, we may well end up disturbing the power elite, or whoever it is that is really in control, without any compensating gains to such a degree that we end up worse off? This is one thing that worries me about the decision made by Judge Garrity. I really have a terrible feeling that—

DR. GREEN: Don't press for redress of legitimate grievances because you might anger the power elite in this nation?

DR. PATTERSON: No, I'm saying, don't press that *way*, don't press that *way*. In other words, attack the power elite the only effective way you can—that is to say, make the gains within the corporate structure—

DR. GREEN: The courts are the most legitimate structure within the corporate structure.

DR. PATTERSON: However, we've exhausted most of them. We've become counterproductive, it seems to me.

MR. MORGAN: With the exception of fourteen years, the courts in the United States ordinarily and almost always have been on the side of the rich, the well-born, and the able. Granted, the courts did strike down the symbol of school desegregation. But after that, everything we won was won exactly as you suggest, by moral suasion, by blacks going into streets, by Rosa Parks refusing to get up on a bus, by Martin King—for whom and with whom Bob worked and on whose board I served in the South. Always remember this. The courts and the Congress of the United States merely ratified a movement set in motion by individuals—nonviolent citizens—a movement which had already been ratified by a majority white population.

DR. TROTTER: To conclude this portion of the program, I would like each of you to answer a question. Precisely what should be our nation's policy on integration and the schools? What stand should we take if we're going to do the kind of job we should with desegregation?

MR. MORGAN: May I go first? Just desegregate across the board, use as little busing or disruption as possible, pair schools—using whatever the techniques are—and wind up with white and black folks going to school together, both in the ghettos and in the suburbs.

DR. GLAZER: I oppose mandatory busing except in cases where segregation is a result of state action—which I don't think is primarily the situation in the North. I assert that unequivocally, I can defend that, and I have defended that. Segregation is not the result of state action in the North, and if it's not the result of state action, I think the state has no goddamn business getting in there and saying, "You, black, go there, because you're black," and "You, white, go there, because you're white."

I think it's a great idea for the races to mingle, to know each other, to advance, and I think we ought to use every possible voluntary means to bring that about.

MR. MORGAN: Fourth of July picnic?

DR. GREEN: First, I fully support the point of view that American schools should be desegregated along race and class lines.

Second, I strongly disagree with Professor Glazer's argument that northern states have not willingly and collectively participated in actions to bring about segregated public schooling. There is a body of data that's available to support that point of view, and I would be willing to share that with him. I have a definitive paper on northern school desegregation, well researched, which clearly illustrates the role of county and state officials, as well as city officials, in bringing about segregation as we know it in northern urban communities.

DR. PATTERSON: First of all, we should begin to define our objectives more clearly and specify what the economic as opposed to purely educational objectives should be.

We should then recognize how the implementation of these objectives will vary from one part of America to another. This is a vast continent. Perhaps this impresses me even more as someone who grew up on a tiny island. This is a huge country and a highly heterogeneous country. One objective may exist in one situation, but may not exist in another; or one may find that in one area the social objectives have already been obtained, but the economic and educational have not, and so on. One should be very careful to specify what the objectives are for particular areas and also be more flexible in the choice of means.

Third, it's important always to be aware of the costs involved in implementing a program. And what worries me is a certain degree of dogmatism which is involved.

Finally, one should also be aware of the fact that this whole issue is an exercise in superstructural play, which I think has reached the limits of its potential. We are running the risk of diverting energies which perhaps we should start to redirect toward the problem of reducing the structure of inequality in American society.

DR. TROTTER: Our four panelist have treated us to an informative and provocative exchange, and they are now ready to field questions from the experts and members of the press in the audience. First question?

BRUCE FEIN, attorney, Department of Justice: I have a question for Mr. Morgan.

In response to Dr. Glazer's concern about court decisions that hinge on racial groups proliferating—because the notion of equality has a tendency to expand and have a difficult time containing itself—you mentioned that, really, this problem was simply a matter of shifting the burden of proof to defendants to show discrimination in certain discrimination cases arising in the South.

But, in fact, in *Keyes* v. *The Denver School Board*, and I believe in *White* v. *Regester* the Supreme Court recognized Mexican-Americans as a special group entitled to the same kind of special treatment that blacks were entitled to. And I believe there's a recent case, growing out of a reapportionment issue in New York, in which a group of Jews is claiming entitlement to special representation in the legislature because they are a minority that has been discriminated against in the past.

In my view, your answer really wasn't responsive to what appears to be a growing trend toward legal recognition of ethnic groups. This trend may, in fact, encourage proliferation and divisiveness in the country, because each group will divide itself under the notion that this will give its members greater legal protection than would otherwise be the case. You, yourself, having dealt with the equal protection clause of the Fourteenth Amendment—which was initially designed specifically to help blacks—know how difficult it is to contain these kinds of legal concepts of equality.

I would like your response on what you think ought to be done, or what could be done, to contain the problem of divisiveness caused by recognition and protection of additional special ethnic groups.

MR. MORGAN: First of all, let's take your term "containing"—you referred to containing the problem. Equal treatment under the law is not exactly the plague, except in Washington. And it's not particularly the plague to the average citizen in the United States for people to be treated equally under the law, regardless of who they are—except, I might add, to the Nixon Department of Justice.

Now, with respect to the fact that the Thirteenth, Fourteenth, and Fifteenth amendments were written peculiarly for blacks and for slaves—to rectify the problems of slavery—that's going to dislocate some white folks.

In fact, it is not a recent outgrowth of the Thirteenth, Fourteenth, and Fifteenth amendments, and especially the equal protection clause of the Fourteenth, to apply those rights to other ethnic groups. They were applied to the Chinese in the 1880s, in *Yick Wo* v. *Hopkins;* they were applied to corporations in the United States in 1886.

I, personally, got the first application of the equal protection clause to the rights of women—in a case that grew out of the Civil Rights movement. Would I favor that use of the amendment as a matter of social policy? As a lawyer, certainly. As a citizen, do I think we should be required to amend the Constitution to include corporations, if we want to call them persons? Sure, I do. Would I include them in the law from this point on? No. But are they there? Sure. Is divisiveness caused by ethnic interpretations of the amendment a problem? Of course not.

DR. GLAZER: Could I make a one-sentence comment on that? The issue is not, to my mind, the expansion of the equal protection clause. The issue is the total distortion of the notion of equal protection to impose on people what to them is not equal protection. To the Chinese of San Francisco, it is not equal protection to be spread all over the city.

MR. MORGAN: When they couldn't run a laundry there were equal protection grievances.

DR. GLAZER: That's right. But they did not want—

MR. MORGAN: Fine. When they get something, it is equal protection, but when somebody else gets something, it's not. That's an absurd conclusion.

DR. GLAZER: They were being treated as an abused minority when they weren't one. And it wasn't equal protection for the people with Spanish surnames who didn't want to be moved out of the Mission District.

JAMES FARER, National Council for Black Child Development: My question I direct to Dr. Green and to the panel in general.
 Earlier you spoke of basic facts and data. My question is, do the basic facts indicate that busing improves education, or do they show that busing only helps bring racial groups together?

DR. GREEN: Typically, when that question is posed, we look at two areas: One, hard-core academic achievement, improvement in basic skills, reading, math and social studies, and, two, attitudes.
 The limited data that we have suggests, on the balance, that there is, over time—if youngsters are placed in a desegregated setting for a long period of time—an overall beneficial, positive impact on the development of democratic attitudes.
 There's been some conflicting data on the effect of busing on academic achievement. But I think much of the recent data—data from Berkeley, California, and from Pontiac, Michigan, as an example—suggest that white academic achievement does not decline and, in some instances, increases, and that black academic achievement typically improves very rapidly and is facilitated by the process of desegregation.
 That, basically, is what the facts suggest. There are a number of complicating factors, one major one being essentially this: It's very hard to get good, accurate data

in settings that are highly flavored with conflict. The testing of black and white youngsters in Boston today would yield a very inaccurate measure of a stable attitude, and the measurement of a stable attitude is key in social science research. One might be measuring fear, anger, hostility, and not really how a black youngster views white children, white people at large, or how a white youngster views black youngsters at large. So, social scientists have not been afforded the luxury that natural scientists typically have, the luxury of carefully controlling their experiments.

But I think the limited data that we have available to us suggests that on the balance desegregation is positive and healthy. It sure has been the case, on the other side of the ledger, in the South, because white attitudes toward blacks in southern communities, rural and urban, have changed dramatically. Even though whites stated that they would strongly be opposed to desegregation in public facilities and that it would bring about a real calamity in the South, once the law was clear and once it was clear that the law would be enforced, there was very little difficulty, and there has been since then a healthy improvement in attitudes of black toward white and white toward black in southern communities. Finally, part of the difficulty in a city like Boston, where there has been a tremendous amount of conflict, is that there has been some hesitancy to strongly enforce the law. This, coupled with the statement by the President that he, himself, did not believe in busing, undermined the effectiveness of the court order and also undermined the willingness of the public at large to support the law.

In other words, law and order is hard to enforce when the public perceives that key and powerful political leaders are not supportive of the law.

DR. TROTTER: But I think the statement was made that we do have to support the law.

DR. GREEN: I think that statement was made, and I do believe that court-ordered desegregation is appropriate and should be obeyed.

CHARLES DONEGAN, Howard University School of Law: It seems to me that Dr. Glazer's position is that he would agree with the Supreme Court's majority opinion in *Plessy* v. *Ferguson*, in which it was held that separate but equal facilities did not violate the equal protection clause of the Fourteenth Amendment. But we're also mindful of *Brown* v. *Board of Education*, decided in 1954, which said that separate but equal was inherently unequal and violated the equal protection clause.

With respect to his preoccupation, in my opinion, with voluntarism, it was held in *Green* v. *County School Board*, decided in 1968, that freedom-of-choice plans would have to be discarded because they were not instrumental in abolishing segregated schools. Also, in *Swann* v. *Charlotte-Mecklenburg Board of Education*, decided in 1971, the Court said that busing was permissible.

My question to Dr. Glazer is, does he think it's up to the individual citizen to determine which laws they will comply with and which ones they will not?

DR. GLAZER: There are quite a few points there. First, I do not agree with the Supreme Court decision in *Plessy* v. *Ferguson*. Nothing I have said should have suggested that I agreed with the separate but equal decision of *Plessy* v. *Ferguson*. That decision upheld state laws separating the races. I attack any kind of law making racial distinctions. Let me make that perfectly clear.

Second, I support the *Brown* decision, absolutely, totally, and completely.

Third, I support the *Green* decision. But the *Green* decision on voluntarism has nothing to do with the situations I am talking about. The voluntarism the *Green* decision attacked was not a true voluntarism. There had been a black school determined by law and a white school determined by law. Then the county had said that anyone could go to the school they wanted to, but the blacks were not allowed, by violence and intimidation, to go to the white school, and the whites didn't go to the black school. That was a fake voluntarism.

The voluntarism of the North is not a fake voluntarism. METCO is not a fake voluntarism. The voluntarism that permits free choice in many northern cities is not fake. Blacks, when they choose schools, aren't driven out by rocks and stones, and their parents are not threatened and do not lose their jobs. That's not the case in Hartford, that's not the case in Rochester, it wasn't the case in New York, and it isn't the case in the Boston area.

Finally, just as I oppose the *Plessy* v. *Ferguson* decision on separate but equal and would have felt it was perfectly within my rights as a citizen to attack that decision and to believe that in time the Court would come to its senses and would agree that that decision was in error, so I oppose the decision of the Court in *Keyes* in Denver, and so I oppose the upholding of the decisions in San Francisco and in Pasadena. These are wrong decisions. They take situations in which a partial concentration of the races exists for a variety of reasons and distort that situation into a finding of state-induced segregation.

The Court is wrong in these cases. There will be new appointments to the Court, I hope, and the Court will discover it was wrong, just as it discovered it was wrong in the case of *Plessy* v. *Ferguson*.

MR. DONEGAN: Excuse me, but Dr. Glazer did not seem to answer my question. My question was, is it up to individual citizens to determine which laws or judicial decisions they will comply with and which ones they will not?

DR. GLAZER: It is not up to the individual citizen to determine that, but the individual citizen, while obeying the law, has the right to protest the law—certainly you would agree with that—has the right to argue with the law, while obeying it; has the right to organize and to present evidence that the law in this case is wrong; he has the right—

DR. GREEN: Peacefully.

DR. GLAZER: —peacefully—has the right to hope that, in time, the law will be changed to accord with his view as to what the proper law in that connection is.

EDWARD O'CONNELL, Office of Representative Richardson Preyer: Dr. Green, in the Detroit situation, with the *Milliken* decision having said there is no interdistrict remedy to that problem, is not the only solution left for the suburban districts and the Detroit school districts to cooperate, voluntarily, so as to integrate those schools? Isn't that the only thing left?

DR. GREEN: No. I think there is another option available there. The Court did not definitively rule out the possibility of metropolitan desegregation. What the Court stated was essentially this: that unless proof can be given that the suburban school districts in some way were responsible for segregated policies in urban centers, desegregation will not be mandated by the courts. So I think the burden of proof rests with the plaintiff, or the NAACP, in that setting.

Again, knowing Michigan—my colleague, Mr. Morgan, said I was a southerner, and I have lived and worked in the South, but I was born and raised in Detroit, attended the Detroit public schools, and served as the expert witness in the case there and—

MR. MORGAN: I only knew you when you went straight. [Laughter.]

DR. GREEN: —and analyzed much of that data. I've had an opportunity, in other words, to understand the cultural milieu throughout Michigan. And I can assure you, sir, that voluntary desegregation between Detroit and Grosse Pointe, Detroit and Warren, Detroit and Oak Park, and the surrounding fifty-seven suburban school districts will not occur. The whites who moved to the suburbs and worked cooperatively with the officials of other suburbs to ring Detroit are not likely now to look for ways to voluntarily bring blacks to their districts. And, for sure, they will not voluntarily send their children to the Detroit public school system.

So I support voluntarism. My wife is a volunteer serving on numerous committees—brings no money home, but she's a good volunteer. [Laughter.]

DR. GREEN: Voluntarism typically is an approach recommended by those who wield power. We cannot put the burden of voluntarism on the hundreds of poor racial minorities in school districts throughout the United States of America.

MR. O'CONNELL: Then your solution would be to go to the courts in all the major center cities, rather than to the suburban districts?

DR. GREEN: My solution would be to encourage and support METCO and all of the other volunteer approaches. For example, I strongly supported the voluntary desegregation of restaurants in the South; when the storeowner had the willingness and the foresight to desegregate his store in the South, I supported that.

But we also utilize the judicial approach to speed the process up. I'm saying that I have yet to see the evidence, and I am still looking for someone to provide me with the evidence, that voluntarism has had a real impact on educational policy nationally. I'm not ruling voluntarism out. I support it. But I think the courts are as yet the best instruments of social change—not the worst, as Professor Coleman and Professor Glazer and others have indicated. I see the courts as being relatively cautious, relatively conservative, relatively concerned with collecting data and carefully analyzing that data and reaching good, careful conclusions and recommendations, in most cases.

VALERIE EARLE, Georgetown University: I have two questions, both for Mr. Morgan and Dr. Glazer.

First, you said, Mr. Morgan, that *Yick Wo* was an early example of extension of the equal protection clause to other than blacks. The new kind of equal protection—which is, I think, what is concerning Mr. Glazer and me—is one under which many suspect classifications are developing. I share Mr. Glazer's concern about "quotas, quotas, quotas." And I don't find your early history about juries or *Yick Wo* very comforting on this point and would welcome further comment.

Second, why is it that public policy has not moved to a vigorous effort against redlining? Why must school busing or other such means be the instrument of attack upon segregation in residential facilities? Why not legislation on redlining? Why the schools?

MR. MORGAN: On redlining, to take the last question first—fine. I think we should move against it, and I think the courts should move against it. I do not, for instance, see the courts as the be-all and the end-all. I am interested in changing the judges on the courts in order to make sure that we get even better rulings in this area.

Yes, we should move on redlining. But let me add, Dr. Earle, I have heard all of my life we should move on education whenever we're moving on unemployment; and whenever somebody moves on unemployment, then they are told to move on housing. And whenever we move on housing, we are told "educate first"; if we educate first, they'll be able to get jobs, and if they get jobs, they'll be able to live in the housing, and if they can live in the housing—well, it's all some sort of a circle. The only thing to do is to take whatever part of the circle you can and go forward.

DR. GLAZER: Well, I think Dr. Earle is sort of on my side, so I won't really say anything but that I agree that the trend of "quotas, quotas, quotas" has serious implications. I'm worried about where it's going.

On redlining—sure, I'm against it. But I must say, there, redlining has its own problems—banks don't want to lose their money, and so forth.

But whatever we can do to break down the practices, we should do. That is certainly one area of real concern we should look into.

MR. MORGAN: And I want to add, also, you're talking about *Yick Wo* and more recent applications of the Fourteenth Amendment—even under the antislavery Thirteenth Amendment, protection was provided to Spanish-speaking people. The whole practice of peonage was a substitute form of slavery which was outlawed by interpretation of the equality amendments.

So I don't think that new problems are presented. Of course the courts are asked to solve some problems that I, personally, do not believe they are the most competent instruments to solve. Nor do I believe, second, that lawyers or judges by their nature will come to the same conclusions that I—as an individual citizen who still trusts in the people, including juries and voters—would come to.

JAMES WILLIAMS, Staff, House of Representatives: Mr. Morgan, I'm concerned about how you would determine which students would be bused from the ghetto to the middle-class neighborhood and which students would be bused from the middle-class neighborhood to the ghetto or to the upper-class neighborhoods. In seeking group or social class equity, I wonder how you would handle the question of individual equity?

MR. MORGAN: I'll take, first, your group and social class equity. I don't see the principal problem as being only the exclusion of blacks from the public schools. I think what we have developed in this country is a single, and dual, and then a quadruple, class system of education, whereby in white suburbs 99 percent of the children in old Hogwash High go to college. Well, 99 percent of those kids' daddies or mothers went to college; they're rich, upper middle-class kids, who go from there to Harvard, where they set up a quota to bring a few blacks in voluntarily.

Now, to achieve equity we can use something called the alphabet—A through Z. I would decide who goes where by assigning children equally—in alphabetical order. I would use the alphabet in this wonderful little community that we've got over here of rich white folks, and in the terrible, terrible little community over there of poor black folks. Once those rich white folks' kids get in that black folks' school, guess what's going to happen? The windows are going to get fixed, the police are going to be in the neighborhood, the school is suddenly going to be a quality school, the film of this discussion is going to be shown there, and the money is going to come from the board of education. That's what the answer to integration is. White folks aren't going to put their money into anything their children don't go to, and black folks wouldn't if they had the money.

DR. GREEN: I once participated in a weekend seminar involving a group of so-called "power whites" and some concerned blacks brought together to talk about desegregation. I never will forget a very distinguished, well groomed white woman from Grosse Pointe who said, "I will never allow my child to attend a rat-infested school in Detroit with broken windows." She was married to a very influential lawyer from Grosse Pointe. Later in the day, she had an insight. "Aha," she said, "if my child were bused into that rat-infested school with broken windows, I'd move in there and those windows would no longer be broken, and the rats would run."

DR. PATTERSON: Isn't there another solution? It seems to me we're assuming the continuation of the rather peculiar system of support for education which exists in this country—the quite unique and, I think, rather backward system that is based on local real estate taxes. Wouldn't that problem you're talking about be solved by having a centralized system of support for education?

DR. GREEN: This is what metropolitan desegregation is about. We're speaking about the sharing of resources, along with desegregation. Keep in mind that boundaries that separate cities are not magically determined; they're politically determined. And communities that have political lines separating them share power, and they share all sorts of resources. And we're trying to extend that resource to include human beings, simply put.

MR. WILLIAMS: Mr. Morgan, I'm troubled by this. Are you suggesting that you would expect me to willingly comply with a law which told me that I should send my children to a school other than the neighborhood school, simply because my last name was Williams—that I should somehow accept an arrangement under which my children were bused to a school two or three miles away and the children of the neighbor next door, whose name began with "A," could go to the neighborhood school?

Do you really think a rational man need accept that kind of explanation for a law that looks at that as equity?

MR. MORGAN: Let me put it to you this way. Do I think that you and I, both white folks, think that if we lived in a society as a minority where black folks had the power and the money, and we were put off in some ghetto school, do we really believe that those black folks would put a sufficient amount of money into your school and mine to make sure that our kids got an equal education? I don't happen to believe they would.

Second, I believe that we ought to get around in this country to doing some things under the equality clauses of the Thirteenth, Fourteenth, and Fifteenth amendments —that whole thrust of law—to make sure that when people are charged with crimes, they get an equal representation; to make sure that the rich folks don't get out of jail; to make sure that the rich folks don't get out of sending their kids to the poor folks' schools, to make sure that the poor folks get the advantages of the rich folks, so that everybody gets a fair start in this country and that it's not just a few that wind up with advantages because their parents had a little something going for them, or because they might have been a little bit smarter than somebody else.

Your question is, do I expect you to accept it—no, I don't. Do I care—no, to that also.

DR. GREEN: To reverse the question, furthermore, if your neighborhood school did not have proper science equipment, had an inferior reading laboratory, and your youngster could be bused one-and-a-half miles away to receive top-flight, quality instruction, which would allow him to graduate from high school, to attend Harvard, and then become employed by the House of Representatives, would you allow your child to be bused? That's the question.

DR. GLAZER: By the way, neither Professor Patterson nor I attended Harvard. I went to City College in New York, myself. In addition, Harvard doesn't have a quota on blacks.

MR. MORGAN: "Are you now, or have you ever been. . ." [Laughter.]

DR. GLAZER: Right. We just happen to teach there. Let me just say that I fully agree with Professor Patterson's point that you can do a good deal with money, even though some of my Harvard and non-Harvard colleagues have argued otherwise.

Moreover, it is not the case on the whole that the schools black people go to are very poorly funded compared to schools that white people go to. That's not the case. It's not the case in Boston, it's not the case in New York. Now, it is also true that, even though the black schools are not more poorly funded—we've had studies showing that—their needs are nevertheless greater. I think we have to put more money into them; I quite agree on that. But let's not live under the illusion that the average black in this country has less spent on his schooling than the average white; the amounts turn out about the same.

DR. GREEN: You know, I'm amazed by the kind of data that's being accumulated at Harvard University. Would you dare argue that the quality of education provided, and the amount of money spent, in suburban communities surrounding Detroit, surrounding Gary, Indiana, surrounding Atlanta, Georgia, is commensurate—

MR. MORGAN: It's the whole tax base. The Supreme Court ruled on that.

DR. GLAZER: We have evidence on that. Not all suburbs are rich suburbs; a lot of industrial suburbs surround those cities. Central cities on the whole are spending easily at the national average or above it, and central cities are the place where most blacks live. We don't want to get into the detailed figures here, but I assure you it cannot be shown that the average expenditure for black students in this country is less than that for white.

What can be shown is that the average expenditure for the children of the poor people in this country is less than the average expenditure for the children of rich people. That is so tremendously clear that there's no question about it.

DR. GREEN: And the bulk of the black community is poor.

DR. GLAZER: But the bulk of the blacks live in central cities, where expenditures for education are relatively high.

DR. TROTTER: The whole thrust, I might stress, of the goals as far as the federal government is concerned is to make educational expenditures more equitable.

MR. MORGAN: Let me say one more thing. Mr. Williams, who asked a question a moment ago, works for folks in Congress who represent constituencies, and a lot of us in a sense represent constituencies. It seems to me that all of us, everybody in this room, could do a better job representing those constituencies if, in our lives, we had grown up knowing a lot more about poor people and about the kinds of problems they have than we do.

And as for that child with a name starting with "W" or "M" who lives on one side of town and is bused across town to a school in a poorer section, most children don't learn from a Professor Glazer, a Professor Patterson, a Professor Green, or even me—and I have taught, too. They learn from their fellow students. Members of Congress make more than $40,000 a year, and all federal judges and top federal officials make more than $40,000 a year, which happens to be $27,500 more a year than what the average family in this country has to live on. I think we'd all be better off if we knew how those poorer folks lived.

EUGENE MORNELL, U.S. Commission on Civil Rights: I have two brief questions for Dr. Glazer. First, Judge Garrity in Boston found that the Boston School Committee had, for a long period of time, deliberately and calculatingly segregated the schools of Boston. Judge Real in Pasadena found the same thing about the situation there.

Other judges in northern cases found the same thing. Are you disagreeing with their findings after a review of the evidence, or are you simply disagreeing with their decisions?

My second question is, how do you stand on the proposition that if we want a segregated society, we should have segregated schools; if we want a desegregated society, we should have desegregated schools?

DR. GLAZER: On your first question, I've looked at the evidence, and I disagree with the decisions. Those schools were not segregated by state action. Without going into details, let me just say that sometimes judges err, on the basis of evidence brought to them—sometimes there's only one side in a suit, like in the case of San Francisco where no one was arguing the opposite side.

On your second, I can't answer a rhetorical question. I want a desegregated society and desegregated schools. But what we're really talking about here are the definitions of the words segregation and desegregation. I think it was a sad moment when the word segregation—which means, to my mind, the setting apart of a group on the basis of intent—came to be used to describe situations where, basically, there was no intentional setting apart.

To answer your question without using those loaded words, as I feel you have used them—yes, I want a society in which there is more and more equality among groups, and I think we're moving in that direction; I also want a society in which there is more and more contact among groups, and I think we're moving in that direction, too. But I don't think the best way of moving in that direction is to assign equal proportions of every race and ethnic group, under the threat of legal action, to every situation in the country.

MICHELLE CHARGOIS, National Council for Black Child Development and Howard University: Since the members of the panel can't agree on busing, I'd like to hear about alternatives. It seems to me that a basic issue is not so much whether black children go to school with white children or other racially or ethnically different children, but whether there is discrimination in the allocation of resources to schools whose students are mostly minority children. In this connection, I would like to refer Dr. Glazer, particularly, to a 1971 article on school expenditures in New York City.* The article suggested that, despite local and state statutes requiring equal allocation across schools, school officials had made discriminatory allocations to schools with majority white populations, majority Puerto Rican populations, and majority black populations.

I would like to hear suggestions from the panel about new strategies for funding school systems, as well as about other strategies for reducing the effects of discrimination.

DR. GREEN: I agree that a fair allocation of educational resources is imperative. But that alone is not adequate to ensure that all young people—black, white, irrespective of social class—receive what I would define as quality education.

In my view quality education involves two things, the development of adequate skills in areas related to academic achievement and, equally important, the elimination or modification of negative attitudes and the building of positive attitudes towards race and social class. Even if funds were equally allocated across racial groups, quality education would never get off the ground in a society that's race conscious, as long as racial isolation or racial identity is maintained. This is true, first because individuals who wield power are not going to reallocate that power and distribute it evenly across the board; Gulf Oil is not going to do it, Standard Oil is not going to do it, and the American public school corporation is not going to do it. Second, I hold to the position that as long as this nation is race and class conscious, separate but equal will not stand the test of a fair distribution of funds economically in this country.

DR. PATTERSON: I think one of the basic problems is just how one goes about improving relations between the

---

* Editor's note: Annie Stein, "Strategies for Failure," *Harvard Educational Review*, vol. 41, no. 2 (May 1971), pp. 158-204.

races. The often-made assumption is that improvement will come about through direct contact among the young, the school children. And there is some evidence that it does.

But there is another way, one that America hasn't tried yet. The other way is this: If black kids come from homes beset by the factors that generate a lack of racial dignity—factors such as having unemployed fathers, living in bad neighborhoods, growing up in the kind of setting that's known as the "street culture"—it seems to me that before we bring kids together and say, "Relate," we ought to ensure that the kids coming together have the necessary degree of self-dignity. Once that self-dignity is ensured, direct contact will be much easier.

So, I think, the thing has been turned around in this country. A good case can be made for the fact that bringing together blacks and whites at a time when there are such radically different kinds of factors determining their conceptions of themselves may well intensify insecurities in the relationship of one to the other. Self-dignity should precede direct contact.

MR. MORGAN: Let me mention one thing. First, with respect to the other non-black minority groups in the United States, a great number of those people had parents who were literate. They may have been literate in Polish, or in Russian, or in German, or in some other language. But they were literate and had been literate for generations.

In this country, we forbade blacks to be literate. We made it a crime for them to be literate, and we even put whites in jail for teaching blacks to be literate. And we went from that to generation after generation of segregated schools, unequal schools, impoverished with respect to funds and everything else.

Now, given that circumstance, whatever system you choose for integrating your school system—pairing maybe being preferable to busing—but whatever the system is, it just ought to be done—outright! It doesn't really matter whether it's buses. Of course, the parents may not want their kids bused. But you know, we don't give children one heck of a lot of rights, anyway.

DR. PATTERSON: Let me respond with another question which concerns me. Assuming adequate resources, are blacks incapable of creating an ideal school setting? There seems to be a certain kind of racial pessimism running through your argument—and I'm not arguing here for racial segregation. I'm just saying that, too often, it is assumed that the only way in which there can ever be improvement in the quality of black education and in the quality of relations between the races is through direct contact between whites and blacks. I worry about that.

MR. MORGAN: That's not my assumption.

DR. GREEN: That's not the key. I think you really have not heard me clearly. You mentioned you were from a small island. I would assume that that island was predominantly black; is that the case?

DR. PATTERSON: Yes.

DR. GREEN: Okay. I clearly have made the point several times that the island that you come from hopefully is in a position—should be in a position, and I would argue, indeed, that it can be in a position—to structure a quality education—

DR. PATTERSON: It wasn't when I was growing up; it was a colony.

DR. GREEN: Okay. Well, there are those who argue that blacks are a colony within the United States.

MR. MORGAN: Did you get your freedom in a discussion over coffee, at a human relations council meeting?

DR. GREEN: Let me continue to address that point. Power structures in America—powerful athletic clubs, country clubs, congressional caucuses, and the like—operate to effectively prevent blacks from building the kind of quality educational system that you refer to.

DR. PATTERSON: But if they're so powerful, how can you ever hope to—

DR. GREEN: Well, you have to utilize a number of strategies. We found, for example, that there is a good American tradition of being willing to obey and consider the law; that, we know.

Second, we do know that collective social groups, country clubs, women's groups, have not brought about change in public policy in America. We also know that the religious community has not made a profound impact upon policy; the church has simply failed.

Third, the courts have clearly been able to bring about a tremendous amount of change in this nation. This is not to suggest that policy is made by the courts alone.

Finally, it's important to bring young people—black, white, brown—together very early in life, because if you try to bring them together as young adults and assume they're going to relate, then we might miss the boat.

I would assume that black and white kids at Harvard University are probably more alike than black and white kids across the country who are not in universities and colleges. But at the Harvards, at the Michigan States, you still find the black cultural centers, the white rooms, the ethnic societies, and this phenomenon is related to the fact that we don't begin the process early in life.

MR. MORGAN: And let me just point out that recently a black was elected president of the student body at the University of Alabama. I submit to you that white folks can and have changed their attitudes. Whether change came in Alabama from watching blacks like Calvin Culliver and Willie Shelby playing college football or from something else matters less than one central fact: change came only after blacks took their own rights.

DR. GREEN: Today black and white basketball players at the University of Alabama are even using the same shower. And Wallace said that would never happen.

MR. MORGAN: And I watched that team beat Providence at Madison Square Garden. [Laughter.]

DR. PATTERSON: In other words, you are saying there has been an increase in black—

DR. TROTTER: What we're doing is preempting the audience from participating. I think we have time for one more question.

PETER FURTH, student, University of Rochester: My question is addressed to Dean Green or anyone else who wants to tackle it. Where there has been compulsory racial integration, whether it is through busing or other means, what has its impact been on the quality of education and on the other social goals that one wants to achieve?

DR. GREEN: As I indicated earlier, we are beginning to accumulate data that, hopefully, will suggest that policies of desegregation, first racial desegregation and then integration as the next step, will have a long-range positive impact on American public education. I think the limited data that we have from such communities as Pontiac, Michigan, and Berkeley, California—taking just two examples, one on the West Coast and one in the Midwest—suggest that the policy of desegregation does not lead to long-range conflict. Second, the data suggest that if parental groups, adult groups, do not interfere and foment discontent, young people can learn together and the environment can become a very healthy and productive one from an educational standpoint.

DR. TROTTER: Ladies and gentlemen, this concludes another Public Policy Forum presented by the American Enterprise Institute for Public Policy Research. I'd like to thank you very much for your participation, and to thank particularly the members of this very distinguished panel. [Applause.]

Design: Pat Taylor

## ROUND TABLES

**The Economy and Phase IV** ($2.00)
John T. Dunlop, Charls E. Walker, Yale Brozen, and Gary L. Seevers

**Foreign Trade Policy** ($2.00)
William R. Pearce, Al Ullman, Barber B. Conable, Jr., and Hendrik S. Houthakker

**Watergate, Politics, and the Legal Process** ($2.00)
*Part One:* Charles S. Hyneman, Richard M. Scammon, Aaron Wildavsky, James Q. Wilson, and Ralph K. Winter, Jr. *Part Two:* Richard M. Scammon, Harry H. Wellington, James Q. Wilson, and Ralph K. Winter, Jr.

**Indexing and Inflation** ($2.00)
Milton Friedman, Charls E. Walker, Robert J. Gordon, and William Fellner

**Japanese-American Relations** ($1.50)
Hubert H. Humphrey, Ted Stevens, Robert S. Ingersoll, and Philip Caldwell

**Health Insurance: What Should Be the Federal Role?** ($2.00)
Bill Brock, James C. Corman, Al Ullman, and Caspar Weinberger

**Affirmative Action: The Answer to Discrimination?** ($2.00)
Owen Fiss, Richard Posner, Vera Glaser, William Raspberry, and Paul Seabury

**Government Regulation: What Kind of Reform?** ($2.00)
Hubert H. Humphrey, Ronald Reagan, Hendrik S. Houthakker, and Ralph Nader

**Freedom of the Press** ($2.50)
Floyd Abrams, Edward J. Epstein, William B. Monroe, Jr., Jack Nelson, Kevin P. Phillips, Antonin Scalia, Charles Seib, Clay T. Whitehead, and Ralph K. Winter, Jr.

**The Financial Crisis of Our Cities** ($2.00)
Hugh Carey, Jacob Javits, Sidney Jones, and Charles Percy

**Reforming Federal Drug Regulation** ($2.00)
Michael J. Halberstam, William N. Hubbard, Jr., Louis Lasagna, Gaylord Nelson, and Alexander M. Schmidt

Round Tables are also available in audio-video cassettes. For information contact AEI.

**Busing: Constructive or Divisive?** engages experts in
sociology, and education in a broad consideration
controversial public policy issue: busing as a mean
achieve racial equality in the public schools. The dis
sion centers around the fundamental questions of whe
busing is an effective way to desegregate the schools
improve race relations and whether busing has, in fac
positive impact on the quality of education.

The panel, moderated by Virginia Trotter, assis
secretary for education at the Department of Health,
cation and Welfare, includes Nathan Glazer, professo
education and sociology at Harvard University, Rober
Green, dean of the College of Urban Development at M
gan State University, Charles Morgan, director of
Washington office of the American Civil Liberties Ur
and Orlando Patterson, professor of sociology at Har
University. Dr. Green and Mr. Morgan share the view
busing is a necessary remedy to a complex problem,
that it is and has been an effective tool in improving
cational quality. Professors Patterson and Glazer, v
stressing the importance and success of voluntary de
regation, argue that the policy of forced busing as follo
by the federal government and the courts has often
counterproductive in terms of educational quality, b
advancement, and racial and social harmony.

$2.00

**American Enterprise Institute for Public Policy Researc
1150 Seventeenth Street, N.W., Washington, D.C. 2003